PRINCEWILL LAGANG

Emotional Intelligence in Love

First published by PRINCEWILL LAGANG 2023

Copyright © 2023 by Princewill Lagang

All rights reserved. No part of this publication may be reproduced, stored or transmitted in any form or by any means, electronic, mechanical, photocopying, recording, scanning, or otherwise without written permission from the publisher. It is illegal to copy this book, post it to a website, or distribute it by any other means without permission.

Princewill Lagang asserts the moral right to be identified as the author of this work.

First edition

This book was professionally typeset on Reedsy.
Find out more at reedsy.com

Contents

1. Introduction to Emotional Intelligence in Love — 1
2. Understanding Emotional Intelligence — 4
3. Self-Awareness: The Foundation of Emotional Intelligence — 7
4. Empathy: Navigating the Emotional Landscape of Your Partner — 10
5. Self-Regulation: Managing Emotions in Relationships — 13
6. Effective Communication: The Intersection of Emotional... — 16
7. Social Awareness: Reading Emotional Cues — 19
8. Relationship Management: Using Emotional Intelligence to... — 22
9. The Power of Emotional Intelligence in Conflict Resolution — 25
10. Emotional Intelligence and Intimacy — 28
11. Cultivating Emotional Intelligence Together — 31
12. The Journey of Emotional Intelligence in Love — 34

1

Introduction to Emotional Intelligence in Love

Love is a complex and powerful emotion that has captivated humans for centuries. It is the driving force behind many of our actions, decisions, and aspirations. But in the realm of relationships, love alone is not always enough to sustain a deep and lasting connection. This is where the concept of emotional intelligence comes into play. In this opening chapter, we will embark on a journey to explore the profound interplay between emotional intelligence and love, delving into how emotional intelligence enriches and strengthens our connections with others.

Understanding Emotional Intelligence
Before we can fully appreciate the impact of emotional intelligence on love, it's important to grasp what emotional intelligence entails. Emotional intelligence, often abbreviated as EQ, refers to the ability to recognize, understand, manage, and effectively use our own emotions as well as the emotions of others. It encompasses a wide range of skills, from self-awareness and empathy to communication and conflict resolution.

As we navigate the intricate landscape of relationships, emotional intelligence becomes a guiding compass, enabling us to navigate the ebbs and flows of emotions that inevitably arise. It equips us with the tools to identify and interpret not only our own feelings but also the feelings of our partners, fostering a deeper sense of connection and mutual understanding.

The Relevance of Emotional Intelligence in Relationships

In an era where the pace of life is frenetic and the demands on our time and attention are relentless, emotional intelligence takes on a new level of significance. As we forge connections with others, be it romantic partners, family members, or friends, our ability to attune to their emotional states becomes paramount. The capacity to listen actively, offer genuine support, and validate their feelings lays the foundation for meaningful and lasting relationships.

But why is emotional intelligence particularly crucial in the context of love? Love, after all, is often portrayed as a powerful and all-encompassing emotion that transcends all barriers. However, love's potency alone does not guarantee the harmonious coexistence of two individuals. Emotions can be intense and volatile, and without the ability to comprehend and manage them effectively, misunderstandings and conflicts can arise, potentially eroding the very love that brought individuals together.

Enhancing Love Through Emotional Intelligence

Emotional intelligence enhances love by fostering emotional intimacy, trust, and resilience. When partners possess a high level of emotional intelligence, they are better equipped to create a safe space where vulnerability is embraced and emotional barriers are dismantled. This environment nurtures a sense of emotional closeness, allowing individuals to share their deepest thoughts, fears, and desires without fear of judgment.

Moreover, emotional intelligence enables effective communication, which is the lifeblood of any relationship. The ability to convey emotions, needs, and concerns in a clear and empathetic manner reduces misunderstandings and prevents conflicts from escalating. By empathetically tuning into each other's emotional states, partners can address issues with compassion and find mutually agreeable solutions.

In summary, this chapter serves as a foundation for our exploration of the intricate relationship between emotional intelligence and love. As we continue our journey, we will delve deeper into the specific components of emotional intelligence, its role in different types of relationships, and the practical strategies for enhancing emotional intelligence to create more fulfilling and enriching connections with our loved ones.

2

Understanding Emotional Intelligence

Defining Emotional Intelligence and its Components
Emotional intelligence is a multifaceted construct that encompasses various skills and abilities crucial for understanding and managing emotions, both in oneself and in others. At its core, emotional intelligence involves the capacity to perceive, assess, express, and regulate emotions in a healthy and adaptive manner. This chapter delves into the key components of emotional intelligence and their role in shaping relationship dynamics.

1. Self-Awareness: Self-awareness forms the foundation of emotional intelligence. It involves recognizing and understanding one's own emotions, as well as the triggers that elicit these emotions. A partner with high self-awareness can identify their emotional state, acknowledge its influence on their thoughts and behaviors, and take steps to manage it effectively.

2. Self-Regulation: Building on self-awareness, self-regulation involves the ability to control and manage one's emotions, particularly in challenging situations. This skill prevents impulsive reactions driven by negative emotions and allows individuals to respond thoughtfully and constructively.

In relationships, self-regulation leads to more productive discussions and prevents conflicts from escalating.

3. Empathy: Empathy is the ability to understand and share the emotions of others. It involves putting oneself in another person's shoes and perceiving the world from their perspective. In romantic relationships, empathy enables partners to connect on a deeper level, as they genuinely understand each other's feelings and experiences.

4. Social Skills: Social skills encompass effective communication, conflict resolution, and collaboration. These skills are essential for building and maintaining healthy relationships. Individuals with strong social skills can navigate tricky conversations, express their needs, and listen actively to their partners. These abilities foster open lines of communication and create an environment of mutual respect.

Recognizing the Impact on Relationship Dynamics

Emotional intelligence has a profound impact on the dynamics of relationships. Partners who possess high emotional intelligence are more likely to experience positive outcomes in their interactions and connections. Here's how emotional intelligence influences relationship dynamics:

1. Communication: Effective communication is at the heart of any successful relationship. Emotional intelligence enables individuals to express themselves clearly, listen actively, and validate their partner's emotions. This skill prevents misunderstandings and ensures that both partners feel heard and understood.

2. Conflict Resolution: Conflicts are inevitable in any relationship, but emotional intelligence provides the tools to manage disagreements constructively. Partners with high emotional intelligence can address conflicts without resorting to blame or criticism. Instead, they focus on understanding each other's viewpoints and finding compromises that strengthen their bond.

3. Intimacy and Trust: Emotional intelligence fosters emotional intimacy by creating a safe space for vulnerability. Partners who understand and validate each other's emotions build trust and a stronger connection. They can share their thoughts and feelings openly, leading to a deeper emotional bond.

4. Emotional Support: In times of stress or challenges, emotional support is crucial. A partner with emotional intelligence can provide the needed comfort and empathy, helping their loved one navigate difficult situations with resilience.

Conclusion

Understanding emotional intelligence and its components is vital for comprehending the intricacies of relationships. By recognizing the impact of emotional intelligence on relationship dynamics, individuals can actively work on enhancing their own emotional intelligence to cultivate healthier, more fulfilling connections with their partners. This chapter serves as a stepping stone for our exploration of practical strategies to develop and apply emotional intelligence in the context of love.

3

Self-Awareness: The Foundation of Emotional Intelligence

The Role of Self-Awareness in Fostering Healthy Relationships
Self-awareness, the cornerstone of emotional intelligence, plays a pivotal role in nurturing and sustaining healthy relationships. This chapter delves into the significance of self-awareness in the context of emotional intelligence and explores how it contributes to the overall well-being of relationships.

Understanding Self-Awareness
Self-awareness involves recognizing and understanding one's own emotions, thoughts, and behavioral patterns. It's the ability to take a step back and objectively observe oneself, gaining insight into why certain emotions arise and how they impact interactions with others. In relationships, self-awareness is akin to having a mirror that reflects one's inner world, allowing for greater authenticity and self-reflection.

Fostering Emotional Intimacy
Self-awareness forms the foundation for emotional intimacy in relation-

ships. When individuals are in touch with their own emotions, they can communicate their needs, desires, and concerns more effectively. This openness cultivates an environment where partners feel safe to do the same, creating a reciprocal exchange of vulnerability that deepens emotional connections.

Managing Reactivity

A lack of self-awareness can lead to reactive behavior, where emotions dictate actions without conscious thought. For example, if a partner is unaware of their tendency to become defensive when criticized, they might respond with anger instead of understanding. Self-awareness helps break this cycle by allowing individuals to identify their triggers and choose more constructive responses, fostering a healthier emotional climate.

Techniques for Understanding and Managing Emotions

Developing self-awareness involves honing the ability to recognize emotions as they arise and understanding their underlying causes. Here are techniques that facilitate this process:

1. Mindfulness: Mindfulness involves being fully present in the moment and observing one's thoughts and emotions without judgment. Practicing mindfulness meditation can enhance self-awareness by helping individuals become attuned to their internal experiences.

2. Journaling: Keeping a journal provides a private space to express emotions, reflect on experiences, and identify patterns. Regular journaling can unveil recurring emotional themes and trigger points, aiding in self-discovery.

3. Reflective Practice: After emotionally charged situations, take time to reflect on your reactions and emotions. Consider what prompted those emotions and whether your response aligned with your values and intentions.

4. Seek Feedback: Trusted friends or partners can offer insights into your

emotional tendencies that you might not be aware of. Constructive feedback can shed light on blind spots and contribute to personal growth.

5. Emotional Vocabulary: Expand your emotional vocabulary to accurately label and understand the nuances of your feelings. This practice deepens emotional insight and facilitates effective communication with others.

Conclusion

In the realm of emotional intelligence, self-awareness is the linchpin that sets the stage for growth, understanding, and harmony in relationships. By cultivating self-awareness and applying techniques to understand and manage emotions, individuals lay a solid foundation for enhancing emotional intelligence and creating more fulfilling connections with their loved ones. This chapter sets the groundwork for our exploration of the subsequent components of emotional intelligence and their impact on love and relationships.

4

Empathy: Navigating the Emotional Landscape of Your Partner

Understanding Empathy's Significance in Love and Connection
Empathy, the ability to understand and share the emotions of others, is a vital component of emotional intelligence that plays a central role in fostering love and connection. In this chapter, we delve into the profound significance of empathy in relationships and explore how it contributes to the depth and quality of emotional bonds.

Empathy as a Bridge of Connection
Empathy serves as a bridge that connects individuals on a deeply emotional level. When partners feel understood and validated by each other, a profound sense of connection and intimacy flourishes. Empathy allows individuals to go beyond surface-level interactions and engage in authentic conversations that explore the rich tapestry of emotions that make up their shared experiences.

Validation and Emotional Safety
Empathy creates an emotional safe haven where partners can freely express

their feelings without fear of judgment. When one partner empathetically listens to the other's experiences, emotions, and concerns, it sends a powerful message that their feelings are valid and worthy of acknowledgment. This validation fosters an environment of trust and openness, enabling partners to be vulnerable without reservations.

Enhancing Emotional Intimacy
By attuning to their partner's emotions, individuals can tap into their inner world and comprehend their desires, fears, and joys. This insight lays the foundation for a deeper emotional intimacy, allowing partners to truly see and understand each other. Empathy enables partners to be present for each other, offering support and comfort during challenging times and amplifying the joy during moments of celebration.

Strategies for Practicing Empathetic Listening and Understanding
Practicing empathy involves more than just nodding along; it requires active engagement and genuine understanding. Here are strategies to enhance empathetic listening and understand your partner's feelings:

1. Active Listening: Engage in active listening by giving your full attention to your partner when they speak. Maintain eye contact, nod, and provide verbal cues that show you're present and interested.

2. Put Yourself in Their Shoes: Imagine yourself in your partner's situation and consider how you might feel. This perspective-taking helps you connect with their emotions on a deeper level.

3. Ask Open-Ended Questions: Encourage your partner to share more by asking open-ended questions that invite them to elaborate on their thoughts and feelings.

4. Reflective Responses: After your partner shares their emotions, reflect back what you heard to ensure you understood correctly. This confirms your

engagement and allows for clarifications.

5. Avoid Judgment: Create a non-judgmental space where your partner feels safe expressing themselves. Suspend your own judgments and opinions while they share.

6. Validate Emotions: Acknowledge and validate your partner's emotions even if you don't fully understand them. Let them know that their feelings are respected and appreciated.

Conclusion

Empathy serves as a beacon of emotional connection in relationships, allowing partners to traverse the intricate landscape of each other's emotions. By practicing empathetic listening and understanding, individuals can deepen their bonds, foster emotional intimacy, and create a lasting foundation of trust and love. This chapter propels us forward into exploring the impact of empathy on conflict resolution, effective communication, and the overall vitality of relationships.

5

Self-Regulation: Managing Emotions in Relationships

Exploring the Importance of Self-Regulation in Maintaining Harmony
Self-regulation, a key component of emotional intelligence, is the art of managing one's own emotions in a way that promotes healthy interactions and maintains harmony in relationships. This chapter delves into the vital role of self-regulation in sustaining positive connections and provides strategies for effectively managing emotions, particularly during conflicts.

Maintaining Emotional Balance
In the context of relationships, emotions can sometimes run high, leading to impulsive reactions that may cause harm. Self-regulation enables individuals to navigate the tumultuous seas of emotions with composure and poise. By choosing deliberate responses over knee-jerk reactions, individuals can prevent conflicts from escalating and ensure that conversations remain productive and respectful.

Preserving Open Communication

Effective communication hinges on the ability to express oneself clearly and listen attentively. Self-regulation supports this by preventing emotional outbursts or defensive reactions that might hinder open dialogue. When individuals are in control of their emotions, they can communicate their thoughts and feelings in a way that encourages understanding and connection.

Strategies for Handling Emotions Constructively During Conflicts

Conflicts are a natural part of any relationship, but how they are managed can significantly impact the relationship's health. Here are techniques for practicing self-regulation and handling emotions constructively during conflicts:

1. Pause and Breathe: When emotions start to escalate, take a moment to pause and take a few deep breaths. This brief interlude can help calm your nervous system and provide space for rational thought.

2. Use "I" Statements: Express your feelings using "I" statements to convey your emotions without placing blame. This approach encourages understanding and minimizes defensiveness.

3. Practice Empathy: Before responding, try to understand your partner's perspective. This perspective-taking can help you approach the conflict with empathy and a willingness to find common ground.

4. Time-Outs: If the conflict becomes overwhelming, consider taking a temporary break. Use this time to collect your thoughts, reflect on your emotions, and approach the situation with a clearer mindset.

5. Reflect on Values: Consider whether your reaction aligns with your values and the kind of partner you aspire to be. This reflection can guide you towards responses that promote harmony and connection.

6. Seek Solutions: Focus on finding solutions rather than dwelling on blame

or past grievances. Working together to find resolutions can lead to a stronger partnership.

Conclusion

Self-regulation is a cornerstone of emotional intelligence that enables individuals to manage their emotions effectively, particularly in the face of conflicts. By maintaining emotional balance and practicing self-regulation, individuals can foster open communication, prevent conflicts from escalating, and uphold the harmony of their relationships. This chapter paves the way for our exploration of the final component of emotional intelligence and its role in love and connections: social skills.

6

Effective Communication: The Intersection of Emotional Intelligence and Love

How Emotional Intelligence Enhances Communication in Relationships

Effective communication is the lifeblood of any successful relationship, and emotional intelligence provides the tools to elevate communication to new heights. In this chapter, we explore the profound impact of emotional intelligence on communication within relationships and delve into techniques for expressing emotions, needs, and concerns with clarity and empathy.

Fostering Connection Through Communication

Emotional intelligence enriches communication by enabling individuals to not only convey their thoughts but also understand and respond to the emotions underlying their partner's words. Partners who possess high emotional intelligence are attuned to nonverbal cues, tone of voice, and subtle shifts in emotions, allowing for deeper connections and more meaningful exchanges.

Empathetic Listening and Validation

Emotional intelligence empowers individuals to engage in empathetic listening, where they actively tune into their partner's emotions and offer validation. This active engagement communicates genuine interest and concern, fostering an environment where partners feel understood and supported.

Conflict Resolution with Compassion

Emotional intelligence plays a pivotal role in conflict resolution by fostering a compassionate approach to disagreements. Partners with high emotional intelligence can articulate their emotions and needs while remaining open to their partner's perspective. This ability to express themselves clearly and listen empathetically paves the way for collaborative problem-solving.

Techniques for Expressing Emotions, Needs, and Concerns

Practicing effective communication requires deliberate efforts to express emotions, needs, and concerns in a way that promotes understanding and connection. Here are strategies to enhance communication through emotional intelligence:

1. "I" Statements: Frame your messages using "I" statements to express your emotions and thoughts without blaming or accusing. This encourages open dialogue and minimizes defensiveness.

2. Active Listening: Demonstrate active listening by maintaining eye contact, nodding, and responding appropriately. Show your partner that you are fully engaged in the conversation.

3. Use Empathy: Reflect on your partner's emotions and validate their feelings before responding. This empathetic approach demonstrates your understanding and fosters connection.

4. Choose the Right Time: Select an appropriate time to initiate important conversations. Avoid sensitive topics during moments of stress or distraction.

5. Reflect on Emotions: Before communicating, take a moment to identify your emotions and consider how best to convey them. This introspection can lead to more constructive exchanges.

6. Ask for Clarification: If something your partner says is unclear, ask for clarification rather than making assumptions. This prevents misunderstandings and promotes effective communication.

Conclusion

Effective communication is the linchpin that binds emotional intelligence and love in harmonious unity. By harnessing the power of emotional intelligence, individuals can engage in conversations that nurture connection, empathy, and understanding. This chapter not only highlights the vital role of effective communication but also prepares us for our final exploration of emotional intelligence: its social skills component and how it contributes to relationship dynamics.

7

Social Awareness: Reading Emotional Cues

The Role of Social Awareness in Perceiving Emotions in Others
Social awareness, a fundamental component of emotional intelligence, enables individuals to read and understand the emotions of others. This chapter delves into the crucial significance of social awareness in perceiving emotional cues within relationships and explores strategies for tuning into your partner's emotional state and needs.

Cultivating Connection Through Social Awareness
Social awareness acts as a lens through which individuals can view and comprehend the emotional experiences of their partners. By sensitively tuning into nonverbal cues, facial expressions, body language, and tone of voice, individuals with high social awareness can decipher the unspoken emotions that lie beneath the surface. This skill deepens connection by allowing partners to feel seen and understood on a profound level.

Enhanced Empathy and Understanding
Social awareness nurtures empathy by facilitating a more accurate under-

standing of what others are feeling. When individuals can accurately perceive their partner's emotions, they can respond with empathy, offering the support and validation needed during moments of joy or hardship.

Conflict Prevention and Resolution

In relationships, misunderstandings can often arise due to miscommunication or unexpressed emotions. Social awareness serves as a tool for conflict prevention by enabling partners to detect signs of emotional discomfort early on and address them before they escalate into conflicts. Additionally, during conflicts, partners with high social awareness can recognize when their partner's emotions are escalating, leading to a more empathetic and measured response that de-escalates tension.

Strategies for Tuning into Your Partner's Emotional State and Needs

Developing social awareness involves honing the ability to read emotional cues and accurately interpret the emotional landscape of others. Here are strategies for enhancing social awareness within relationships:

1. Pay Attention to Nonverbal Cues: Observe your partner's facial expressions, gestures, and body language during conversations. These cues can provide valuable insights into their emotional state.

2. Listen Actively: Engage in active listening to not only hear the words your partner is saying but also to understand the emotions behind those words.

3. Ask Open-Ended Questions: Encourage your partner to share their feelings by asking open-ended questions that invite them to elaborate on their thoughts and emotions.

4. Practice Presence: Be fully present during interactions with your partner. Minimize distractions and give them your undivided attention to better understand their emotions.

5. Validate Emotions: When you notice your partner experiencing emotions, validate their feelings by acknowledging them. This creates an environment of understanding and support.

6. Seek Clarification: If you sense that something might be bothering your partner, gently inquire to see if they would like to talk about it. This shows your willingness to engage and support them.

Conclusion

Social awareness serves as a bridge that connects partners on a deeper emotional level. By sharpening the ability to read emotional cues and understand the emotional landscape of their partners, individuals can enhance empathy, prevent conflicts, and foster a heightened sense of connection within their relationships. This chapter leads us to the culmination of our exploration of emotional intelligence within relationships, as we delve into the practical application of these skills for love and connection.

8

Relationship Management: Using Emotional Intelligence to Strengthen Bonds

Applying Emotional Intelligence to Foster Connection and Trust
Relationship management, the final pillar of emotional intelligence, involves using emotional awareness, empathy, and social skills to build and maintain healthy connections. In this chapter, we explore the application of emotional intelligence to strengthen bonds within relationships. We'll also delve into techniques for resolving conflicts, building intimacy, and maintaining a robust and lasting partnership.

Nurturing Emotional Connection
Relationship management centers on fostering emotional connection by creating an environment where partners can express themselves openly and authentically. Emotional intelligence equips individuals with the tools to respond empathetically to their partner's emotions, fostering a sense of trust and intimacy that deepens over time.

Conflict Resolution Through Emotional Intelligence

Conflicts are a natural part of any relationship, but how they are managed can shape the relationship's trajectory. Emotional intelligence enables partners to engage in conflict resolution with compassion and understanding. Techniques like active listening, perspective-taking, and using "I" statements help partners express their feelings, validate each other's emotions, and collaborate towards solutions.

Building Intimacy and Vulnerability

Emotional intelligence paves the way for building emotional intimacy by encouraging vulnerability. Partners with high emotional intelligence can share their thoughts, fears, and desires openly, knowing that they will be met with understanding and support. This level of trust deepens the bond between partners and fosters a more fulfilling connection.

Maintaining a Strong Partnership

Sustaining a strong partnership requires ongoing effort and communication. Emotional intelligence plays a crucial role in maintaining the vitality of a relationship. Partners can continue to practice active listening, empathy, and open communication as they navigate life's challenges and joys together.

Techniques for Resolving Conflicts, Building Intimacy, and Maintaining a Strong Partnership

Effective relationship management involves using emotional intelligence as a guiding compass in various relationship situations. Here are techniques for applying emotional intelligence to these aspects of a partnership:

1. Conflict Resolution: Listen actively, validate emotions, and focus on finding mutually agreeable solutions. Avoid blaming and prioritize understanding each other's perspectives.

2. Building Intimacy: Share your thoughts, emotions, and experiences openly. Practice vulnerability and encourage your partner to do the same.

3. Maintaining Connection: Continue practicing active listening and empathy throughout the relationship. Regularly check in with each other to ensure you're both on the same page.

4. Celebrating Successes: Acknowledge and celebrate each other's achievements and milestones. Show genuine enthusiasm and support for your partner's growth and happiness.

5. Compromise and Collaboration: Approach decisions with a willingness to compromise and collaborate. This promotes a sense of partnership where both individuals feel valued and heard.

Conclusion

Relationship management is the culmination of emotional intelligence applied within the context of love and connection. By leveraging emotional awareness, empathy, and social skills, individuals can navigate conflicts, build emotional intimacy, and sustain strong and fulfilling partnerships. This chapter marks the conclusion of our exploration of emotional intelligence within relationships, leaving us with a toolbox of skills to enhance our connections and create lasting bonds.

9

The Power of Emotional Intelligence in Conflict Resolution

Navigating Conflicts Through Emotional Intelligence
Conflicts are an inevitable part of any relationship, but the way they are managed can profoundly impact the relationship's health and longevity. This chapter delves into the transformative role of emotional intelligence in conflict resolution, exploring techniques to de-escalate disagreements and find collaborative solutions that strengthen connections.

The Role of Emotional Intelligence in Conflict
Emotional intelligence equips individuals with the tools to navigate conflicts with empathy, understanding, and emotional awareness. By recognizing their own emotions and understanding the emotions of their partner, individuals can approach conflicts with a sense of compassion and curiosity rather than defensiveness or blame.

De-Escalating Disagreements
Emotional intelligence empowers partners to de-escalate disagreements

by diffusing heightened emotions and fostering open communication. Techniques like active listening, validation, and using "I" statements allow individuals to express their perspectives without exacerbating tensions. These skills create an environment where both partners feel heard and respected, laying the foundation for productive conflict resolution.

Empathetic Perspective-Taking

One of the hallmarks of emotional intelligence is the ability to take another person's perspective. During conflicts, this skill allows partners to step into each other's shoes, understanding their feelings and motivations. By empathetically considering their partner's viewpoint, individuals can find common ground and work towards solutions that satisfy both parties' needs.

Techniques for Collaborative Conflict Resolution

Applying emotional intelligence to conflict resolution involves utilizing a range of techniques to find common ground and foster understanding. Here are strategies for resolving conflicts collaboratively:

1. Practice Active Listening: Listen attentively to your partner's perspective without interrupting. Show that you're fully engaged in the conversation.

2. Validate Emotions: Acknowledge your partner's emotions, even if you don't agree with their viewpoint. This validation creates an environment of trust and openness.

3. Use "I" Statements: Express your own feelings and needs using "I" statements to avoid placing blame or accusations.

4. Seek Compromise: Approach conflicts with a willingness to find middle ground. Be open to compromising to reach solutions that satisfy both parties.

5. Take Breaks: If a conflict becomes heated, take a break to cool off before continuing the conversation. This prevents escalation and allows for more

rational discussion.

6. Focus on Solutions: Shift the focus from assigning blame to finding solutions. Collaborate with your partner to brainstorm ideas that address both of your concerns.

Conclusion

Emotional intelligence is a guiding light in the intricate landscape of conflict resolution. By applying emotional awareness, empathy, and effective communication, individuals can transform conflicts from sources of tension into opportunities for growth and connection. This chapter empowers us with the tools to approach conflicts with emotional intelligence, fostering understanding and harmony within our relationships.

10

Emotional Intelligence and Intimacy

Exploring the Link Between Emotional Intelligence and Deepening Intimacy

Intimacy is the heart of any profound and lasting connection. Emotional intelligence serves as a powerful catalyst for nurturing emotional closeness and vulnerability within relationships. In this chapter, we delve into the profound link between emotional intelligence and intimacy, and explore strategies for fostering emotional closeness that enhances the depth of connection between partners.

The Role of Emotional Intelligence in Intimacy

Emotional intelligence lays the groundwork for intimacy by facilitating emotional understanding, effective communication, and empathetic connections. Partners who possess high emotional intelligence can navigate the complexities of emotions with grace, creating a safe space for sharing their thoughts, fears, and desires without judgment.

Enhanced Emotional Communication

Emotional intelligence enhances emotional communication, allowing partners to express their feelings and needs with clarity and sensitivity.

EMOTIONAL INTELLIGENCE AND INTIMACY

By understanding their partner's emotions and responding with empathy, individuals create an environment where intimacy flourishes. The ability to listen deeply and validate emotions creates a sense of emotional safety that fosters vulnerability.

Fostering Vulnerability and Trust

Vulnerability is at the core of intimacy. Emotional intelligence encourages partners to open up and share their true selves without fear of rejection. The empathy and validation that come with emotional intelligence provide the assurance that their feelings will be acknowledged and accepted, creating a foundation of trust that deepens intimacy.

Strategies for Fostering Emotional Closeness and Vulnerability

Fostering emotional closeness and vulnerability requires conscious effort and emotional intelligence. Here are techniques to enhance emotional intimacy within relationships:

1. Share Your Emotions: Express your emotions and thoughts openly, allowing your partner to truly understand your inner world.

2. Listen Actively: Engage in active listening when your partner shares their feelings. Offer your full attention and refrain from judgment.

3. Validate Emotions: Acknowledge your partner's emotions and show that you understand their experiences. This validation encourages further sharing.

4. Create a Safe Space: Foster an environment where vulnerability is celebrated and emotions are met with empathy, not criticism.

5. Share Your Hopes and Fears: Open up about your dreams, fears, and vulnerabilities. This level of sharing deepens the bond and allows your partner to know you on a profound level.

6. Be Present: Be fully present during intimate moments, both physically and emotionally. Put away distractions and focus on connecting with your partner.

Conclusion

Emotional intelligence serves as a bridge to deeper levels of intimacy within relationships. By applying empathy, emotional awareness, and effective communication, individuals can foster emotional closeness and vulnerability, creating a connection that transcends the surface and enriches the relationship's foundation. This chapter concludes our exploration of emotional intelligence in love, leaving us with the tools to navigate the intricacies of emotions and connection with wisdom and compassion.

11

Cultivating Emotional Intelligence Together

Approaches to Growing Emotional Intelligence as a Couple
Emotional intelligence isn't solely an individual pursuit; it can be cultivated and nurtured within a partnership. In this chapter, we explore the transformative journey of growing emotional intelligence as a couple and delve into approaches that strengthen emotional bonds and deepen the connection between partners.

Shared Learning and Exploration
Cultivating emotional intelligence as a couple involves embarking on a shared journey of self-discovery and growth. Couples can explore resources together, attend workshops, or engage in discussions that center around emotional intelligence. This shared pursuit not only enhances individual emotional awareness but also creates a shared language and understanding that enriches the relationship.

Practicing Active Empathy
Partners can actively practice empathy towards each other by tuning into

each other's emotions and offering support during moments of vulnerability. Encouraging open conversations about emotions and feelings creates an environment where partners feel safe to express themselves authentically. Through active empathy, couples develop a deeper bond and a heightened sense of emotional connection.

Mutual Reflection and Feedback

Regular reflection and feedback sessions can become a cornerstone of a couple's emotional intelligence journey. These sessions provide a platform for partners to share their emotional experiences, discuss any challenges they face, and offer feedback in a constructive and compassionate manner. This process strengthens emotional understanding and reinforces a sense of partnership.

How Shared Emotional Growth Enhances Love and Partnership

Shared emotional growth has the potential to transform the dynamics of a partnership in profound ways. Here's how cultivating emotional intelligence together can enhance love and partnership:

1. Enhanced Communication: Couples who grow emotionally together develop more effective communication skills, ensuring that emotions are expressed and understood with clarity and empathy.

2. Deeper Empathy: The practice of empathizing with each other's emotions fosters a stronger sense of understanding and closeness, leading to a more intimate bond.

3. Conflict Resilience: Partners with shared emotional growth are better equipped to manage conflicts constructively, addressing disagreements with compassion and the intention to find solutions.

4. Nurtured Intimacy: The shared language of emotional intelligence creates an environment where partners can be vulnerable, deepening emotional

intimacy and trust.

5. Stronger Partnership: As partners support each other's emotional growth, they create a partnership grounded in mutual respect, empathy, and a shared commitment to nurturing their emotional connection.

Conclusion

Cultivating emotional intelligence together elevates the relationship to a new level of emotional depth and understanding. By embarking on a joint journey of growth, partners enhance communication, empathy, and conflict resolution skills, creating a profound and lasting bond. This chapter concludes our exploration of emotional intelligence within the context of love and partnership, leaving couples with the tools to create a resilient and emotionally connected relationship.

12

The Journey of Emotional Intelligence in Love

Reflecting on the Transformative Power of Emotional Intelligence
The journey of emotional intelligence in love is one of profound transformation, offering couples a path towards deeper understanding, empathy, and connection. In this final chapter, we reflect on the transformative power of emotional intelligence within relationships and explore ways to nurture ongoing emotional growth and connection.

The Evolution of Emotional Intelligence in Love
Emotional intelligence evolves as couples progress through the stages of their relationship. From the initial spark of attraction to the establishment of trust and intimacy, emotional intelligence serves as a guiding light that enhances every facet of the relationship. As partners develop emotional awareness, empathy, and effective communication skills, they create a solid foundation for long-lasting love.

Fostering Ongoing Emotional Growth
Nurturing emotional growth is an ongoing endeavor that requires commit-

ment, practice, and patience. Partners can continue to cultivate emotional intelligence by:

1. Practicing Active Listening: Continuously engage in active listening, showing your partner that you value their emotions and experiences.

2. Seeking New Perspectives: Explore different viewpoints and encourage your partner to share their feelings and thoughts openly.

3. Embracing Vulnerability: Continue to practice vulnerability by sharing your emotions, fears, and dreams with your partner.

4. Reflecting and Learning: Regularly reflect on your emotional intelligence journey together, celebrating progress and identifying areas for growth.

5. Revisiting Tools and Techniques: Revisit the techniques you've learned for emotional awareness, empathy, and conflict resolution to ensure they remain integral to your relationship.

Nurturing Ongoing Connection

As emotional intelligence deepens, so does the connection between partners. Nurturing ongoing connection involves:

1. Quality Time: Spend quality time together, engaging in activities that allow for meaningful conversations and shared experiences.

2. Communication Rituals: Establish communication rituals, such as daily check-ins or weekly reflections, to maintain open and consistent dialogue.

3. Affection and Appreciation: Show affection and appreciation for your partner regularly, reinforcing the emotional bond between you.

4. Embracing Change: As individuals grow and evolve, the relationship

must adapt. Embrace change and continue to support each other's emotional growth.

5. Celebrating Milestones: Acknowledge and celebrate relationship milestones and personal growth achievements, reinforcing the value of your journey together.

Conclusion

The journey of emotional intelligence in love is a transformative one that enriches the connection between partners. By reflecting on the power of emotional intelligence, nurturing ongoing emotional growth, and fostering a deep and lasting connection, couples create a relationship that is grounded in empathy, understanding, and love. This chapter marks the end of our exploration, leaving couples with the tools and insights to embark on their own journey of emotional intelligence within the realm of love.

www.ingramcontent.com/pod-product-compliance
Lightning Source LLC
LaVergne TN
LVHW020456080526
838202LV00057B/5993